MW01244178

[Traumatic Brain Injury]

[I was lost, and I found myself]

By [Joel Pruitt]

Book Positioning

1. Your Objectives

How do you want your book to serve your readers? What will they get out of it?

1. My whole reasoning and hope in this book is to increase understanding of the rehabilitative process of the traumatic brain injury.

2. To show how to increase neural sensitivity and progress in cognitive awareness, understanding and balance.

3. I will show you; I myself had a TBI and there is hope.

Imagine it's two years after your book was published, and we're looking back on the results together. **What's the book done for you that made the effort worthwhile?**

1. This book has shows those who have experienced the trauma associated with TBI, families and caregivers how to pull through the learning experience and help the brain to once again process awareness and understanding.

2. This book is a motivation by self proven steps of action from someone who received a severe TBI from an accident.

3. This book has allowed me (brain injury victim) to instill hope and guidance through the process I learned to create amazing positive change.

What is the *single event* that will happen because of the book, that'll cause you to "break out the Champagne" and celebrate?

The single event(s) that can take place to cause celebration is the restoration of the individual(s) who rehabilitate from the TBI; behavioural, socially, circumstantial, and cognitively.

2. Your Audience

I am here to speak to the families, to the caregivers and to the medical community.

Describe a typical person in your Primary Audience (**your avatar reader**). What are they like? Who are they, and where are they in their life?

The person(s) who read this motivational book, the medical personnel, the families and caregivers of the people who are/have endured this behavioral, cognitive/ memory crises. These are the people who are going to learn the avenue(s) for the TBI victim to gain cognitive retention, awareness, balance and a better state of well being.

What **pain is this person experiencing** because they've not read your book?

The pain this person and families are experiencing because they have not listened to better understand is Confused cognition, (memory impairment), anxious behaviors, No impulse control. The person(s) who do Not read this book to listen attentively to understand will not help create the positive change that I am so thankful for.

What **transformation will this person get in their life** because they read and implement your book?

The transformation that truly can/will come to be will either be of small proportion or amazing proportion. What these proper steps of action are done for me is unbelievable, really. It's amazing how you can literally train the brain's cognitive process for the better. We've all heard it and some of us have experienced it (muscle memory). Your brain has a memory, what you must do is train your brain as you train yourself to do cardiovascular/resistance training and transform the cognitive process of those who have injured themselves.

3. Your Idea

In one paragraph (150 words max), describe **what your book is about, who the ideal reader is, and what will they get from the book?**

My book to you is about Brain Injury Rehabilitation from a TBI survivor.. I am writing to you so that you can hear and listen to one who has been there. From one who remembers I believe most all he went through in regard to this behavioral/cognitive impairment. In the beginning, I did not know where I was, or what was going on about me. In the acute stage and 6 months after inpatient at health south rehabilitation I do not recall anything, I was in a coma and then partial coma for awhile after that. My brain began to process information little by little. I began to gain more and more understanding of what was going on about me. My brain slowly began to recalculate somewhat using different brain processes. I had to relearn the reason for motor movement and situational awareness; yes you start learning so simple because that's where your brain begins trying to process I formation once again. I could not read, write, talk, or walk. I really hope you are listening to me, please hear me, I found out how to learn once again. I'm just going to say it- I hope you're listening. I trained my brain to process information properly once again, gain my certifications and specialty. Exercise created the proper process of neural transport. EXERCISE! Yes, Seriously. I did it! I did it all by myself! It's so true. Do you see how rhetorical I am rite now!

What's the **"cocktail party pitch"** of your book? (i.e., the one sentence explanation your ideal reader would actually use to recommend your book to their friends)

We have all heard it time and time again. Exercise is good for you. Exercise is so good for the brain. It creates proper neural processes. You can regain your memory. It is so nice to get back what you have lost, maybe not fully to the extent that it was, but progressive, ya I remember- now I do!

4. Your Book North Star

Write this sentence with your positioning, and make sure this is the book you want to write:

"I will use my book to target [primary audience], by teaching them [book idea], which will lead to my ultimate goal of more [objectives]."

I will use my book to target families and caregivers, by teaching them by first hand knowledge about Brain Injury Rehabilitation which will lead to my ultimate goal of more and better understanding of how to help the brain overtime begin to process information, create understanding and most importantly learning life process.

Chapter Brainstorming

This section is for all your notes and ideas for your book, before you start putting them into the Table Of Contents.

1. Create neural sensitivity and brain process.
2. Retrain the brain however much is needed to understand the life process.
3. Train the brain to learn
4. All brain Injuries are different
5. Learn proper behavioral process
6. Social learning
7. You can do it
8. The acute phase
9. Cognitive impairment, neural capacity
10. Exercise proliferation
11. gaining cognitive balance

Parking Lot

In this section, put all your really good ideas that DO NOT fit in *this* book. You may end up realizing you have one, two, or more books in you. You can write those later; this section is so you don't lose any of those ideas as you write this one.

1. Exercise secrets
2. Train your brain cognitive retention
3. Personality differentiation

Table of Contents

The Accident

Chapter 1: The accident

Chapter Hook	• My personal story
Thesis of chapter	• Yes, I was there
Supporting content	• It was 11:45 PM on October 6th 2004. Joel Pruitt was turning a corner in his vehicle on his way home from work. Joel took the turn too sharply and hit the guardrail which elevated the vehicle 26 feet vertically and 27 feet laterally into the brush and trees. The vehicle had flipped over 7 times before coming to a stop. Joel's lungs had collapsed and he stopped breathing. Joel laid there suspended and unresponsive for 15 minutes. A nurse happened to be passing by saw the wreck and tended to the situation. A helicopter was called but could not touch down in the trees and timbre. The ambulance was contacted. The paramedics tried to get Joel out of the vehicle by cutting the vehicle open and the seat belt was locked. So they cut the seat belt and removed him from the vehicle. Joel was taken to the hospital to the intensive care unit where he was hooked up with a tracheotomy, a feeding tube and whatever else I do not recall. I Joel Pruitt laid in the ICU for 31 days, dormant, unresponsive. I was then moved to inpatient at health south for 6 months. Now I do not recall any of this because my cognition was dead. My cognitive process was not able to understand anything. After the 6 months inpatient at health south I went home. That is when my brain started to gain small amounts of understanding of where I was as well as the situations about me. The place where I slept at night was moved to an open area, not closed off. I remember always being cold and turning the heat up to 83, 85, 87 degrees at night. I recall eating so much especially sugar, it's like my body was calling for it, and I mean a lot at least 2 boxes of ice cream everyday and more boxes of whatever it was. I recall having to be told what not to do in public or not so much what not do but definitely observed. I recall separating myself from family every so often to the basement where the treadmill was and the door to the outside seeing the brick wall down stairs and punching it time and time again. I would punch trees cause it was fun

or not so much fun but my mind was fixated in a combative survival mode and that is what I did, I recall finding the yellow jackets nest and hitting it messing up there home as they usually would sting me around 7-8 times, I did not care it was ok. Yes, I hate saying it but I would hit the dog, it was a pit bull, but I still to this day remember how uncomfortable that dog was to come near me. I don't like talking about this but I must. When a TBI injury occurs and your brain is recalculating the way it must, these Brain Injuries cause such magnified strength. I of course was told, I will never remember, that I had broken the hospital restraints many times. Other people were fine I was not combative toward others at all, I simply could be that way towards objects, that increased strength is also part of the rehabilitative process. I recall catching flies in mid air with my hand cause I could it was so easy. My senses were so exaggerated and extremely strong and let me tell you why. The TBI has taken my sense of smell away, well, unless my senses say I'm going to taste. One time since my injury occurred have I tasted and my senses made me taste so strong because what I put in my mouth was hot and I'm very sensitive to anything hot and I am partially far sided. When one or more of your senses are taken away your other senses are increased. You have seen this with the blind, or if not there have been shown many science documentaries, many people who are blind simply use echolocation so that they can walk freely with understanding of where the objects are around them with simple clicks of the vocal cords. Since one of their senses is not there the body must compensate by utilizing the senses at hand to create awareness. Well my complete sense of smell was taken so my sense of sound was so, so heightened. I'm thinking to myself as I become more explanatory in regard to what I went through "I'm sounding crazy, people are going to not understand" but I know and understand that is not how it is. I'm being completely forth rite about literally what happens when the brain is injured and must recalculate once again. I would sit in a room and listen to the walls crack- they really do my sense of hearing was that magnified.I began to really understand how animals senses are so powerful and simply being amazed at how they function. I remember hearing many times a dog can

	smell over a mile away, now I have such a real understanding. I remember asking myself if I am standing rite. Am I sitting rite? I would always walk into plastic windows and because I could not process that there was an object between me and what I could see through. Through all of this I knew something was simply not rite. This is where I was… (was).
Key reader takeaways	<ul><li>Somehow my brain remembers all that I went through. I believe my brain processed this information because it was simply functioning by different avenues.</li><li>I was starting over.</li></ul>
Callback to Hook & segue to next chapter	<ul><li>I am telling you, from the standpoint of the victim of a TBI, much. It is a complex rehabilitative process.</li><li>Now I would\need to talk to you in regard to acute Rehabilitation.</li></ul>

Chapter 2: Acute Rehabilitation

Chapter Hook	• Learning simple process of life
Thesis of chapter	• Repetition increases understanding
Supporting content	• Repetition increases comprehension. When I began to see, observe situations, observe action, The repetitiveness of whatever I was trying to analyze increased my understanding in time, but there was deferential, (variance in time). Some things were learned more quickly than others. I often recall the frustration or questioning of why I could not remember what I had seen time and time again. • After the TBI, neural capacity can be overloaded quickly. My accident occurred on October 6th 2004 and to this day in 2020 my brain capacity still gets overloaded quickly. Honestly I am not sure exactly why that is, well I do I believe somewhat, and that is the brain never rehabilitates fully. This is truly a lifelong disability. After the injury, it seems like my brain capacity gets worn out from too much Information at once. Some information quickly, some information slowly. So it is essential to take it slow. • I learned and came to understanding by constant repetition. The constant repetitiveness is what I needed over time for my learning to finally become ingrained into my thought process. • You must make it enjoyable, that way we crave and desire to learn and understand more and more as we feel enlightened by newfound knowledge. And I use the word entitled because the knowledge we have found creates rationale, and that in itself is calming. • We all enjoy learning things that we were not sure of or simply did not know about. When relearning a skill, information of whatever it may be, it feels good to the individual who is a survivor of a TBI to know that they themselves learned whatever it may be they did not know or were unsure of. • This acute phase is the initial learning phase. • It is the beginning, that really is as well spoken as I can be at this point.

Stories	<ul><li>At this time in the rehabilitative process while at home, I began to go to the health south Rehabilitation outpatient care. At this time is when I believe I began to gain more cognitive awareness. Situational awareness and lifestyle observation.</li><li>Later in the acute\sub acute rehabilitative phase I went to 2 separate Brain Injury Rehabilitation Facilities. I felt as though I was different than the others about me. I felt as though I was unlike the others around me who I could see were in need of Rehabilitation. What I have e come to learn is that this thought pro res is common and most all of the time the way it is.</li></ul>
Key reader takeaways	The one single thing that increased my understanding, awareness and learning in social situations, in circumstance, and intellectual knowledge so amazingly; it's unbelievable (listen to the way I talk) was exercise proliferation (repetition). <ul><li>I would be up in my room studying, I would see that I was not comprehending what I should, would go down to the basement to walk or jog for 1\2 mile on the treadmill to increase my understanding. It worked every single time, honestly I simply Intrinsically (within me) knew. Yes, it's true.</li></ul>
Callback to Hook & segue to next chapter	<ul><li>I'm learning a simple process to learn and understand.</li><li>I'm exercising my brain to where I can understand, remember, feel Calm and relaxed, "I feel better, I feel pretty good".</li></ul>

Chapter 3: benefits of exercise after Traumatic Brain Injury

Chapter Hook	• My journey has led me to understanding, peace, tranquility- I am so thankful for my lifestyle change
Thesis of chapter	• Proper, safe exercise brought me through the valleys, the rivers, over the mountains- I swam across the lakes.
Supporting content	• In the beginning, I myself personally decided to initiate exercise, I thought and realized that I had to think about the process of exercise. I realized I had to focus on learning and understanding what and how to do simple steps of action. I was beginning to train my brain on how to think as well as how to adjust my thinking to find a solution (problem solve). At first, honestly, it was tough. I remember trying so very hard to understand and implement what is now so simple. • I myself understand the instructions of (tell, show, do) in a safe manner. This train of thought must be established for proper posture, movement, balance and flexibility. • Once safe exercise is established the motion of movement can begin. • TBI survivors who engage in exercise 3 times a week for 30 minute intervals report less depression, improved perception of physical abilities, and increased community integration as compared with TBI survivors who did not exercise (neuropt.org). • Exercise helped my cognition so much. After the injury to my frontal lobe my short term memory in the few beginning years of Rehabilitation was lost, nowhere to be found. I remember placing a glass, a wallet, keys whatever it may be and have no idea where I had just placed the item and it would be right next to me usually at waist level. My memory was that distorted for I believe about close to or even slightly 4 years. Exercise got my brain transmission back. I'm so thankful. • Once exercise is initiated TBI survivors will feel so much better about themselves. Exercise increases dopamine levels In the brain, which decreases stress, depression and helps remove that edgy feeling stress creates. Furthermore it creates the famous "runners-high" because it enhances those feel good transmitters. I, Joel Pruitt am

	addicted to exercise. I am not trying to hide, I admit my addiction has taken hold of me and put me, Joel Pruitt, who laid in the ICU for 31 days waiting to pass at the age of 24 in perfect health at the age of 41. I am so addicted I'm going for a quick mile run and I'll be back. Sorry, I can't control myself, lol, but true. • After simple walks on a daily basis I felt so much better about myself because I accomplished something. My walks felt so good. • The general benefits of exercise? Regular exercise and physical activity may- • •Help you control your weight •Reduce your risk of heart disease •Help your body manage blood sugar and insulin levels •Help you quit smoking •Improve your mental health and mood •Help keep your thinking, learning, judgement skills sharp as you age •Strengthen your bones and muscles •Reduce your risk of some cancers •Reduce your risk of falls •Improve your sleep •Improve your sexual health •Increase your chances of living longer
Stories	• It got to the point everyday I was thankful to be able to go for walks. Later going for jogs cause I could see and feel what it was doing for me in regard to my thinking, feeling, and behavior. Those who experience the TBI injury understand something is not rite, when corrections can be made it is so nice. • A few things I have come to understand as I process through my lifetime rehabilitation is; I have come to learn whether you are a TBI survivor or not, we are always learning. I have come to understand the more I know the more I think to myself I do not believe we know very much at all, there is so much more to know. I try to keep my thoughts more focused and simple instead of complex.
Key reader takeaways	• We have all heard much of what I have written. • For those who have endured a TBI, there is more.

Callback to Hook & segue to next chapter	• The benefits of exercise after a TBI are amazing, please hear me. • We have just uncovered once again the general benefits of exercise which are wonderful for those of us who have suffered a TBI and for all people. In this next chapter I will show you how, I will show you why, the brain is so responsive, and what exercise does for the TBI survivor.

Chapter 4: The increasing of understanding and learning

Chapter Hook	• It gets so much better
Thesis of chapter	• My personal exercise progression after TBI
Supporting content	• My family was told I will never ever run again for the rest of my life. My family was told I have a 50/50 chance of ever walking again after shattering my foot literally all they new to say is like a piece of shattered glass that was later fused with a metal plate and 9 screws to hold it together. • The remarkable, the unthinkable, was about to happen. • I was given a wheelchair so that I may mobilize around wherever I need to be . I was given a walker so that I may one day maybe learn to walk. Now this is not the proper way to act but of course at the time my brain was repairing itself the best it could and in the the beginning after the hospital acute phase and the 6 months inpatient at health south I simply shunned the wheelchair and walker away. In my mind I quickly decided this is not the way it will be. So I started walking on my shattered foot. No matter what I was told or heard I simply wasn't listening and it was of no concern to me because I don't do wheelchairs or walkers, I just ask, I don't need to use that stuff. I have chosen to walk because that is the way it was going to be. Now it is difficult to talk to those who have suffered a TBI, it is simply very difficult for them to focus on what you are saying, why and to bring that phrase spoken to full meaning or really some or much of the time much meaning at all. So from now on I was walking. The neuropathy in my foot and ankle was severe. The way I alleviated the nerve pain was through walking because despite the severe pain- I was walking. • At my time at the brain injury rehabilitation center it was severe then also, around the 4 to 5 year period mark. • I began to go for runs when I left and it got better and better, less and less, soon probably around 6 years later it was over, it finally went away. The arthritis, it was gone. • I exercised myself into amazing health. My cognitive process is back. My short term memory is restored. • My lifestyle has changed only for the better.

Stories	<ul><li>By no means am I saying to TBI survivors, family members and caregivers to do what I did and start walking on your foot/leg that you shattered like a price of glass. You must let the repair take place and then work with a physical therapist and if referred to a personal trainer, to rehabilitate properly. If I restored my cognition in the rite way but my foot and ankle the wrong way. Think about what can be done if done rite and proper.</li><li>I am here to say the injuries may be severe; cognitively, physically, behavioural.</li><li>The reason my brain was able to recalibrate over time was by what is called neuroplasticity. Neuroplasticity from a clinician's view is the ability of the brain to change and heal itself. It is the brain's ability to affect the transmission of information in response to external stimulation. The brain's ability to heal through exercise should bring hope to others like myself who have sustained a brain injury. For those who have not sustained a brain Injury, it can so manifest a greater state of well being, really it does. Balance means so much to neural connectivity. I know that for me, as far as what really helped increase my learning and understanding was witnessing how others acted in life, and honestly in the beginning and after that is how I myself learned on how to do simple tasks.</li><li>There truly always is hope. Never say never, believe in restoration. The benefit that stands out in my mind above all is the progressive build up of self efficacy (self esteem) personal judgement of how well I became able to execute courses of action required to deal with prospective situations. I remember the beginning, my memory did not forget my new learning through exercise because honestly it was so tuff.</li><li>Exercise brought me through the initial baby steps of simply learning how to learn once again. I remember my mind was constantly so confused by the simple things, really so simple. As simple as simple can be. I recall always questioning everything because I did not understand why. Exercise trained my brain to figure out decisions that I later found out I had to make. I soon began to understand little by little that I was walking the way I should, simple ideas such as that.</li></ul>
Key reader takeaways	<ul><li>I started like that from the beginning. I tend to go back to</li></ul>

	the beginning much because I think to myself over and over, "How could I ever get people to understand where I really was and how far I've come because that is something they I don't believe could possibly ever understand. • Exercise has seriously increased my neural connectivity (memory, thinking) not back to the former but by different avenues.
Callback to Hook & segue to next chapter	• I'm going to say it again because I'm proud of where I have come from. • I can walk now, I can talk now, I can run now, I can write now, I can eat food now, I can drink liquids now, I can socialize now, I can work now, I can problem solve now.

Chapter 5: Exercise proliferation and lifestyle change

Chapter Hook	• I'm doing it
Thesis of chapter	• Exercise is changing my life
Supporting content	• In general these are the benefits of exercise • Weight management: Prevent obesity. To maintain your weight the calories you eat and drink must equal the calories burned. • Reduce your risk of heart disease: Exercise strengthens your heart and improves circulation. The increased blood flow raises the oxygen levels in your body. This helps lower your risk of heart disease; such as high cholesterol, and heart attack, regular exercise can also help lower your blood pressure and try triglyceride level. • Help your body manage blood sugar and insulin levels: Exercise can lower your blood sugar levels and help your insulin work better. This can cut down your risk of metabolic syndrome and type 2 diabetes. If you already have one of these diseases exercise can help you manage it. • Help to quit smoking: Exercise may help you quit smoking by reducing cravings and withdrawal symptoms. It can also help limit the weight you might gain when quitting smoking. • Improve your mental health and mood: during exercise your body releases chemicals that help you feel more relaxed which can help deal with stress and refuse your risk of depression as well as alleviate symptoms of depression. • Helps keep your thinking, learning and judgment skills sharp. Exercise stimulates your body to release proteins and other chemicals that improves the structure and function of your brain! Exercise increased my learning potential and taught my brain to learn by new avenues and pathways.
Key reader takeaways	• Strengthen your bones and muscles: Regular exercise can help kids and teens build strong bones. Later in life it can also slow the loss of bone density that comes with age. Doing muscle strengthening activities can help you

	increase or maintain your muscle mass and strength. • Reduce your risk of some cancers including colon, breast, uterine and lung cancer
Callback to Hook & segue to next chapter	• Stop your risk of falls: For older adults, research shows that doing balance and muscle-strengthening activities in addition to moderate-intensity aerobic activity can help reduce your risk of falling. • Increase your chance of living longer: Studies show that physical exercise can refuse your risk of dying early from the leading causes of death like heart disease and some cancers. The benefits of exercise are for everyone.

Conclusion

Chapter Hook	<ul><li>Look, can you see, I'm doing it</li><li>This is for all of those in the world who have sustained a TBI. This is for the families and caregivers to see and hear that the brain can learn once again, it's not only muscle memory, the brain can remember how to learn and understand again.</li></ul>
Thesis of book	<ul><li>Hope</li></ul>
Tie together each chapter's takeaway with overarching theme of book	<ul><li>I was not supposed to survive. I was not supposed to ever run again. Apparently all was lost. We as people tend to have this idea that when something happens to us that involves or causes sudden great damage or suffering that the outcome must be it's all over. Catastrophe is equivalent to death. That is not true.</li><li>When you fall just like I myself fell on October 6th 2004 at 11:45 PM, you pick yourself up, you brush yourself off and you think/say my name is _____, I am better than this, I must continue. I have so much to show others, to do for others, to help others. I'm not done!</li><li>Lifestyle change has made me who I am today. I can now remember, I can now speak, I can now walk/run, I now feel better everyday, I now can interact with others.</li><li>After my personal rehabilitation from the TBI I finished school and became a Personal Trainer, and now am a Weight Management Specialist.</li><li>I now have started my personal business JDP Fitness Management</li><li>I just wrote a boom/documentary.</li><li>Now I am able to show families/caregivers the way, the path, the process that I myself have learned.</li></ul>
Call to Action	<ul><li>Now that you have read what I have written to you, I ask that you take steps of action to help people like me, the brain injured. I want to thank you so much for reading this and I so hope I have helped open the door to a better life for us. I have gained cognitive balance. Do you know who told me to write this book\documentary to help those who have become victims of this injury like myself? Me, myself, and I. I sustained a Brain Injury October 6th</li></ul>

2004 and am here to say there is hope!

Introduction

IMPORTANT NOTE: The Introduction obviously goes FIRST in the book, but we recommend writing it last. Once written, place it first in the book manuscript.

Book Hook	• I have found the way Way
Frame the reader's pain	• In the beginning it is such travesty, you simply do not know or understand what is happening or what could be. Whenever we as a people undergo such difficulty we automatically think of the worst in search of any hope. And I found hope, there is hope, I survived and manifested change in my life. My short term memory was gone; now my short term memory is better, now I can walk, I can run, I can interact with society, I can work. It was and is a long journey, I had to learn to write, talk, read, walk and everything else once again. I really found the way to gain my cognition back.
Frame the reader's benefits	• From what I will exhort to you- the families, the caregivers; I found the way.
	• In the beginning it was "I don't want to have to walk on that treadmill, what's the point. Until one day I thought I would try it out really quick. I did, and the way I felt after a simple walk for a ½ mile was so much better. I liked the way that I felt. It became a daily continuous progression of a slightly longer walk day by day.
	• I began to realize I could remember more, think slightly more clearly. I began to go for little jogs, and that felt really good. I felt so much better.
	• For the individual who has suffered this injury of cognitive, behavioral impairment, by proper exercise; small baby steps in the beginning, exercise creates better thinking and behaviors through increased self esteem.
	• It makes life so much better for us who have endured this trial.
	• You will see, your family member, the person you care for be more relaxed, ready to learn and more at ease in social situations.

	<ul><li>I am so happy somehow I intrinsically (it was inside me) learned about this process so that I am able to help people who have undergone the same type of trial as I myself have.</li><li>I read much of John C. Maxwell's books on how I can process my thoughts for success (how successful people think). One book that helped me learn about the journey I was on is (your roadmap for success). John C. Maxwell's books are exactly what triggered me to learn that all of those times I was failing over and over again, failure is simply a part of success. It is part of the journey. You will hike over mountains, you will swim across lakes, you will detour different avenues. I learned that when I fall, to fall forward and keep pressing forward. Our repetitive failures on our journey to recovery are simply mile markers on our journey which only shows progression. I continue to progress day by day.</li></ul>
Tell them what they'll learn in the book	<ul><li>You will learn how to teach TBI survivors how to feel better everyday. You will see my fellow survivors be able to think and process more clearly.</li><li>You are going to learn and see the hope of rehabilitation and restoration as your family members or those you care for are able to improve alertness, attention and motivation as well as log in new information.</li></ul>
Describe author's background/origin of book	<ul><li>The entire background and origin of this book is from a TBI survivor. Please hear me, "I am not supposed to be here, seriously. Somehow, someway, I intrinsically (with in) new how to correct my thought process flow through exercise. Exercise truly helps everyone's cognition.</li></ul>
Tell them what the book *is* and *isn't*	• What this book is; this book/documentary is Joel Pruitt, a TBI survivor who is not supposed to be here, speaking to the family and caregivers of fellow TBI survivors. I am telling you first hand what we go through and how you can help us in this long drawn out process. I myself found the way to become more calm, relaxed, sociable with better memory and thought process. Please help people like me, exercise changed my life.

Segue to first chapter/Call to Action	• *Are you ready to help instruct family members, those you care for on how to live healthier fuller lives. How to remember, how to interact, how to feel so much better, how to learn, how to behave once again in society; "than please keep reading".*

Made in the USA
Middletown, DE
29 September 2020

20757367R00017